EZ SPC - Statistical Process Control Demystified

Ralph V. Celone

and

Ronald L. Buckley

EZ SPC – Statistical Process Control Demystified

Copyright © 2013 Ralph V. Celone and Ronald L. Buckley

All rights reserved.

ISBN: 1490451889
ISBN-13: 978-1490451886

Published by
Shady Brook Press
14 Shady Brook Lane
Norwalk, CT 06854

DEDICATION

I dedicate this book to Lisa and Veronica whose seemingly endless contributions helped shape this book into the easy to understand manual that it has become.

CONTENTS

	Acknowledgments	i
1	Introduction	1
2	A Brief History	5
3	Variation	11
4	Why SPC?	15
5	Average	19
6	Median	33
7	Mode	39
8	Range	43
9	Histograms	49
10	Standard Deviation	57
11	Specification Limits	65
12	Control Limits	69
13	Sampling	73
14	Control Charts	77
15	Process Performance	97

CONTENTS

16	Process Capability	105
17	Z Score	117
18	Implementation	123
19	A Few Words About FMEA	129
20	Conclusion	135
	SPC Terms and Definitions	139
	Sources	145
	About The Author	147

ACKNOWLEDGMENTS

A special thanks to Ron Buckley, a friend and mentor, who was the impetus that allowed me to write this book.

And a very special thank you to Lisa Celone, wife, friend, and partner in all aspects of my life. It is her original artwork that graces the cover of this book.

EZ SPC – Statistical Process Control Demystified

CHAPTER 1

Ralph V. Celone

CHAPTER 1
INTRODUCTION

All processes generate outputs that must fall within predefined limits of acceptability and all processes have some degree of natural variation. Statistical Process Control is a method to track the variation within a process and allow us to make adjustments before the variation in the process produces a defect.

The results of the work done by Dr. Deming in Japan, and his work here in the U.S. along with others, have clearly demonstrated that Statistical Process Control is a key tool to improve product quality and increase the yield of acceptable parts.

This book is a compilation of the SPC training I have both received and created throughout my career as an engineer and a businessman. It will cover some of the common tools and techniques used to implement Statistical Process Control for various processes in a simple and concise manner.

The goal of this book is to give you everything you need to know to create and maintain an effective SPC program using only the simple mathematical concepts that we were all taught in grammar school.

This book is divided into three basic sections. The first section contains the tools and techniques needed to understand and create control charts. The second section covers the interpretation of control charts. The third section contains other information necessary to create and maintain a robust SPC program.

Microsoft Excel® has become ubiquitous in just about every business. Throughout this book, you will find that I have included many Excel® functions that help to automate many of the calculations. I have also created an Excel® file that demonstrates all of the functions referenced in this book. This file can be downloaded free of charge from http://www.rlbuckley.com.

There are other statistical analysis software packages (like Mintab® http://www.minitab.com) available that are more focused on statistical analysis, but Excel® can be used quite effectively for the purposes and techniques described in this book.

CHAPTER 2

Ralph V. Celone

CHAPTER 2
A BRIEF HISTORY

Statistical Process Control or SPC began back in the 1930's when a Dr. W. A. Shewhart applied the control chart to an industrial process. When WWII broke out, SPC was introduced to many industries and mandated by the U.S. government on wartime contracts. By utilizing these basic quality control techniques, the U.S. was able to produce military hardware in large quantities at minimum cost. Some of the standards and techniques developed by the Allied powers were so effective, that, at the time, they were classified as military secrets.

Shortly after the war ended, interest in SPC started to decline in the U.S. At that time, the U.S. was the largest producer in the world of quality goods and merchandise. The manufacturing abilities of most other industrialized countries involved in the war had essentially been destroyed by wartime bombing activities. These war torn countries were producing poor quality goods as quickly as possible to bolster their economies. As a result, the U.S. had essentially no competition in the World Market and was able to sell everything produced without the need to improve quality.

For a variety of reasons, industry began to organize around functional areas of expertise as espoused by the then popular Taylor Concept of Scientific Management. Quality Control departments devolved into basic inspection functions where the approach to controlling quality was through defect DETECTION after the fact rather than defect PREVENTION using Statistical Process Control.

Japan's economy, in particular, suffered tremendously because of the inferior goods they were producing. The Union of Japanese Scientists and Engineers (JUSE) was privately formed, and in 1949 established the Quality Control Research Group (QCRG). The main objective of the QCRG was to engage in the research and dissemination of quality control knowledge.

In 1950, the JUSE invited Dr. Deming to visit Japan and participate in a seminar on Quality Control. Dr. Deming began working with Japanese scientists, engineers, and top management, teaching them the basics of SPC and developing an attitude where Quality Control was to be regarded as a management tool. In 1954, Dr. J. M. Juran joined Dr. Deming's efforts in Japan.

By the mid 1960's, Japanese quality and productivity had improved to the point where names like Mitsubishi, Toyota, Kawasaki, and Yamaha were regularly appearing on the World Market.

By the late 1970's, Japan had improved to the point where they were a serious player on the World Market and the U.S. was losing its market share at an alarming rate.

In 1950, Dr. Deming introduced the PDCA diagram pictured here to the JUSE. He called it the Shewhart Cycle after its creator, Dr. W. A. Shewhart. It soon became known as the Deming Cycle or PDCA cycle.

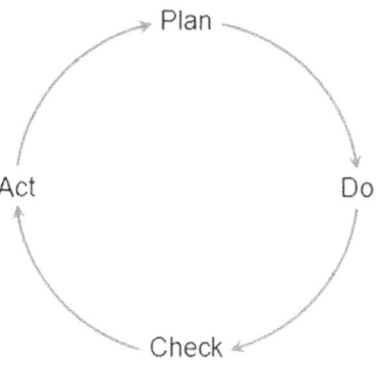

The PDCA cycle graphically demonstrates the steps we use every day to manage both our lives and our businesses.

Ralph V. Celone

CHAPTER 3

Ralph V. Celone

CHAPTER 3
VARIATION

Please note that every process has what is called "normal" or "random variation".

Variation is the root cause of ALL process defects. If our processes were robust enough to eliminate variation, every part would be identical to every other part produced every day of production.

Some of the causes of variation are: changes in raw material, machine wear, tool wear, and human variation and error.

We will learn how to use SPC to quantify and minimize variation and to identify trends that indicate our processes are no longer operating as desired before the processes produce defects.

Ralph V. Celone

CHAPTER 4

Ralph V. Celone

CHAPTER 4
WHY SPC?

SPC is used to identify changes that are occurring in a process BEFORE the process changes enough to create defects. This is one of the most important SPC concepts to remember as it will enable you to save time, money, and run your process with minimal defects.

The goal of a Lean program is to reduce waste. One of the causes of waste is variation. The goal of a Six Sigma program is to reduce variation. In this way, Six Sigma can be thought of as a subset of Lean and an extension of SPC.

A complete Six Sigma program will provide many data analysis tools to teach your people to study and analyze your process data in many, many different ways. It also provides a standardized format for trouble-shooting issues. However, it does rely heavily on higher level math and statistics and is generally beyond the level of education of the most typical operator. It can also build bureaucracy and inertia into driving changes because of what is referred to as "analysis paralysis". Your people spend so much time analyzing data that the actual process improvements are needlessly delayed.

While many businesses do opt to implement a full-blown Six Sigma or a Lean Six Sigma quality improvement plan, the costs and efforts associated with those programs can be astronomical when compared to a simple SPC rollout, which will bring essentially the same benefits.

I have created this book based on my career experiences, and to fill a void between Six Sigma and the production floor. I have used the techniques described in this book to train operators who never graduated High School and/or speak English as a second language to become expertly proficient in the simple math required, and to be able to create and interpret Control Chart data and to alert others of impending problems before the process begins producing defects.

If you want to maximize your investment, my advice is to get a decent SPC program up and running effectively and then consider more education intensive programs for key individuals.

CHAPTER 5

Ralph V. Celone

CHAPTER 5
AVERAGE

The Average, Mean or $\bar{x}$ (pronounced x bar) or μ (pronounced mu) are all used interchangeably as names for the same concept. The average is simply the sum of a series of measurements in a sample divided by the number of items measured (the number of items measured is sometimes called the number of observations). Mathematically it's written as

$$Average = \frac{x_1 + \cdots + x_n}{n}$$

For example, let's say we measured the amount of time it took for a customer's phone call to be answered at a call center and we measured the following:

Measurement #	Time (Minutes)	Measurement #	Time (Minutes)
1	0.84925	26	0.85010
2	0.84925	27	0.85000
3	0.84930	28	0.84965
4	0.84890	29	0.84970
5	0.84875	30	0.84965
6	0.84875	31	0.84995
7	0.84820	32	0.84990
8	0.84845	33	0.84975
9	0.84835	34	0.84815
10	0.84825	35	0.84825
11	0.84860	36	0.84825
12	0.84795	37	0.84920
13	0.84815	38	0.84900
14	0.84850	39	0.84925
15	0.84855	40	0.84830
16	0.84915	41	0.84710
17	0.84875	42	0.84815
18	0.84910	43	0.84880
19	0.84945	44	0.84875
20	0.84935	45	0.84860
21	0.84940	46	0.84850
22	0.84995	47	0.84880
23	0.84945	48	0.84870
24	0.84975	49	0.84855
25	0.84975	50	0.84850

If we add up all 50 measurements, we get 42.44685 minutes and if we divide 42.44685 by 50, we get 0.848937 minutes as the average response time. With this information, we can estimate, that for any caller, the average time for their call to be answered will be 0.848937 minutes or about 51 seconds.

For a sweeter SPC application, consider a group of friends who all purchased bags of M&M® candy. Frank, Al, Dave, Greg, and Tom all sorted their M&Ms® by the various colors and counted the number of candies of each color. Their counts are summarized in the table below.

Name	Orange	Red	Green	Blue	Yellow	Brown	Total
Frank	17	9	7	18	3	4	58
Al	17	3	9	12	3	7	51
Dave	18	6	8	8	4	8	52
Greg	12	3	10	20	4	6	55
Tom	16	10	7	18	4	1	56
Average	16	6.2	8.2	15.2	3.6	5.2	54.4

A sixth friend joining the group, and taking a random bag of M&Ms®, can be pretty sure that they will have about 54 pieces of candy and that will consist of about 16 Orange, 6 Red, 8 Green, 15 Blue, 3 Yellow, and 5 Brown candies. I encourage you to try this one yourself.

For some additional practice, refer to the accompanying Excel® file called EZ SPC.xlsx and look in the tab called Mean.

The Excel® function to calculate the mean is "average". It can be used to return the average of a column of numbers, a row of numbers, a table of numbers, or a series of individual numbers as demonstrated in the following graphics.

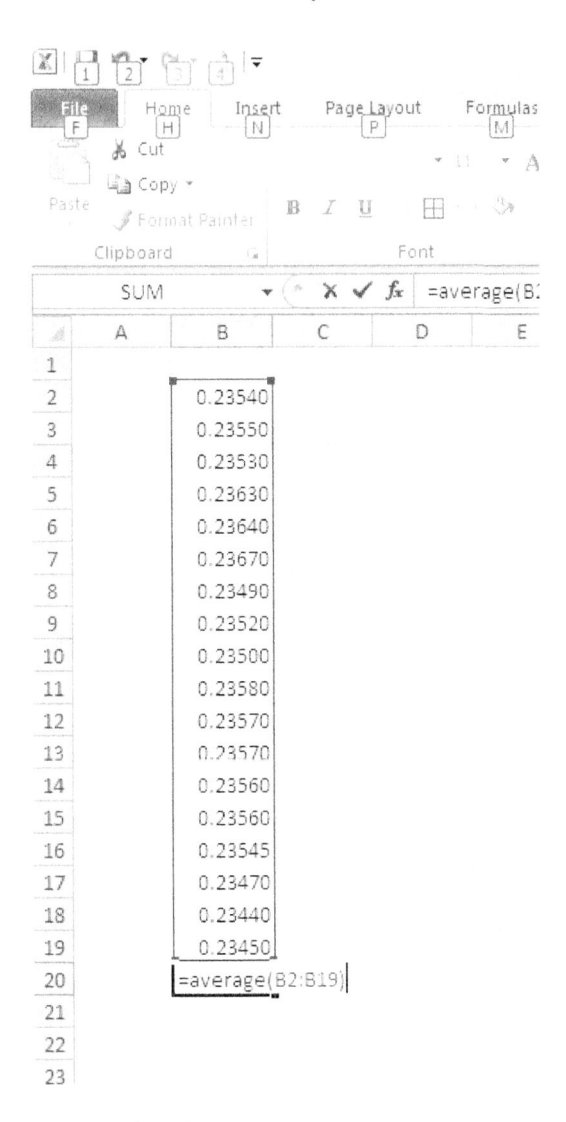

	A	B	C	D	E
1					
2		0.23540			
3		0.23550			
4		0.23530			
5		0.23630			
6		0.23640			
7		0.23670			
8		0.23490			
9		0.23520			
10		0.23500			
11		0.23580			
12		0.23570			
13		0.23570			
14		0.23560			
15		0.23560			
16		0.23545			
17		0.23470			
18		0.23440			
19		0.23450			
20		=average(B2:B19)			
21					
22					
23					

Average of a Column

EZ SPC – Statistical Process Control Demystified

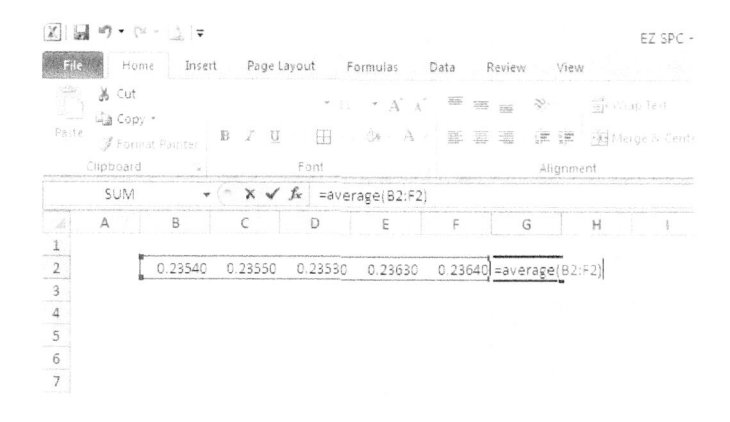

	A	B	C	D	E	F	G	H
1								
2		0.23540	0.23550	0.23530	0.23630	0.23640	=average(B2:F2)	
3								
4								
5								
6								
7								

Average of a Row

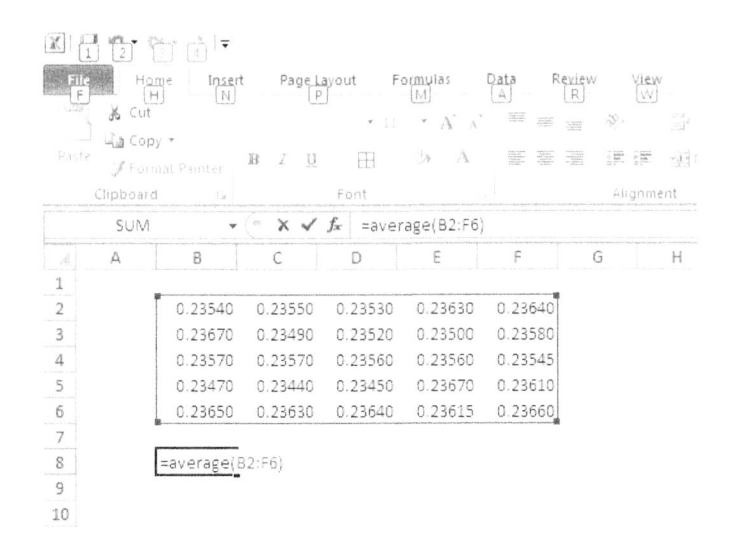

	A	B	C	D	E	F	G	H
1								
2		0.23540	0.23550	0.23530	0.23630	0.23640		
3		0.23670	0.23490	0.23520	0.23500	0.23580		
4		0.23570	0.23570	0.23560	0.23560	0.23545		
5		0.23470	0.23440	0.23450	0.23670	0.23610		
6		0.23650	0.23630	0.23640	0.23615	0.23660		
7								
8		=average(B2:F6)						
9								
10								

Average of a Table

EZ SPC – Statistical Process Control Demystified

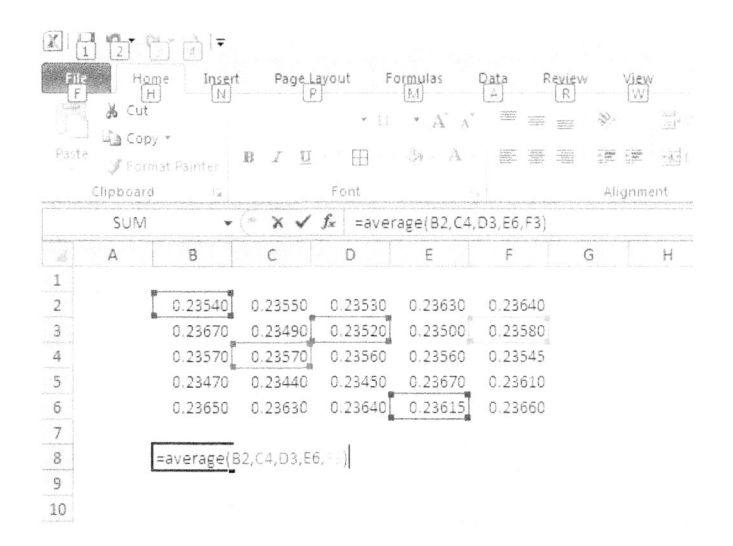

	A	B	C	D	E	F	G	H
1								
2		0.23540	0.23550	0.23530	0.23630	0.23640		
3		0.23670	0.23490	0.23520	0.23500	0.23580		
4		0.23570	0.23570	0.23560	0.23560	0.23545		
5		0.23470	0.23440	0.23450	0.23670	0.23610		
6		0.23650	0.23630	0.23640	0.23615	0.23660		
7								
8		=average(B2,C4,D3,E6,F3)						
9								
10								

Formula bar: =average(B2,C4,D3,E6,F3)

Average of Individual Numbers

What we all call the Average is really the Arithmetic Mean. It is part of a family of three means called the Pythagorean Means. The other two members of the family are the Geometric Mean and the Harmonic Mean. Chances are that you will never need to use the Geometric or Harmonic means in your everyday SPC work, but, I am including them in this book for completeness.

Recall that the equation for the Average is:

$$Arithmetic\ Mean = \frac{x_1 + \cdots + x_n}{n}$$

The equation for the Geometric Mean is:

$$Geometric\ Mean = \sqrt[n]{x_1 * \ldots * x_n}$$

Lastly, the equation for the Harmonic Mean is:

$$Harmonic\ Mean = \frac{n}{\frac{1}{x_1} + \cdots + \frac{1}{x_n}}$$

As an example, given the dataset:

$$[1, 2, 3, 4, 5, 6, 7, 8, 9, 10]$$

the Arithmetic Mean is 5.50
and the Geometric Mean is 4.53 (rounded)
and the Harmonic Mean is 3.41 (rounded).

However, given the dataset:

$$[1, 2, 3, 4, 5, 6, 7, 8, 9, 100]$$

the Arithmetic Mean is 14.50
and the Geometric Mean is 5.70 (rounded)
and the Harmonic Mean is 3.52 (rounded).

The Arithmetic Mean will always have the largest value of the three Means. The Harmonic Mean will "favor" the smaller numbers and always be the least of the three means. The calculation for the Geometric Mean tends to "normalize" the data being averaged, reducing the effects of outliers as shown above. The Geometric Mean will always be somewhere between the Arithmetic Mean and the Harmonic Mean.

The Arithmetic Mean (or Average) is generally the calculation most used to study quantities – for example, red M&Ms® per bag or wait time per call.

The Geometric Mean is used mostly to study rates of growth or rates of return as in a financial situation. The Geometric Mean also tends to "normalize" outliers and variation in large or different data sets.

For example, if I made an initial investment of $100 and the first year earned 3% interest, 2% the second year, and 6% percent the third year, what was my average rate of growth during those three years? After Year 1, I have $103 – my growth rate for that year was 1.03. After Year 2, I have $105.06 – my growth rate for that year was 1.02. At the end of Year 3, I have $111.36 my growth rate for that year was 1.06.

I could calculate an average growth rate of:

$$Avg = \frac{1.03 + 1.02 + 1.06}{3} = 1.0367 \ (Rounded)$$

But, if I multiply that out as shown below:

$$100 * 1.0367 * 1.0367 * 1.0367 = 111.41$$

I incorrectly get $111.41 as my total holdings at the end of Year 3.

However, I can calculate the Geometric Mean using the same numbers, and get:

$$GeoMean = \sqrt[n]{x_1 * \ldots * x_n}$$

$$GeoMean = \sqrt[3]{1.03 * 1.02 * 1.06} = 1.0365281 \ (Rounded)$$

Multiplying that out gives me the following:

$$100 * 1.0365 * 1.0365 * 1.0365 = 111.36$$

Which correctly calculates the actual amount I have after three years.

The Harmonic Mean is used mostly to study average quantities such as speed during an automobile trip. For example, if I drove 100 miles in two hours, my average speed was 50 miles per hour. If I then drove another 100 miles in four hours, my average speed was 25 miles per hour. If I use the Arithmetic Mean, my average speed for the trip is incorrectly calculated as:

$$Average = \frac{50 + 25}{2} = 37.5 \; mph$$

But, I spent six hours on the road and covered 200 miles – the correct average speed is 33.33 mph. Plugging the speeds into the Harmonic Mean equation, I correctly calculate:

$$Harmonic \; Mean = \frac{2}{\frac{1}{50} + \frac{1}{25}} = 33.33 \; mph$$

Like the Average (Arithmetic Mean), Excel® also has functions for the Geometric and Harmonic means. The functions are "geomean" and "harmean" and they are used in the same way as the "average" function.

Ralph V. Celone

CHAPTER 6

CHAPTER 6
MEDIAN

The Median is sometimes confused with the Mean. However, they are two separate concepts. While the Mean is the average of a group of measurements, the Median is the one measurement that separates the upper half of the measurements from the lower half of measurements. If there are an even number of measurements, the Median is the average of the two middle measurements. This concept is illustrated in the following table.

2	2
3	3
4	4
5	5
9	6
Median value is 4	9
Mean value is 4.60	Median value is 4.5
	Mean value is 4.83

The Excel® function "median" will determine the median of a group of numbers. Like the "average" function, it can be used on a column of numbers, a row of numbers, a table of numbers, or a series of individual numbers. The next figure demonstrates the use of the "median" function.

EZ SPC – Statistical Process Control Demystified

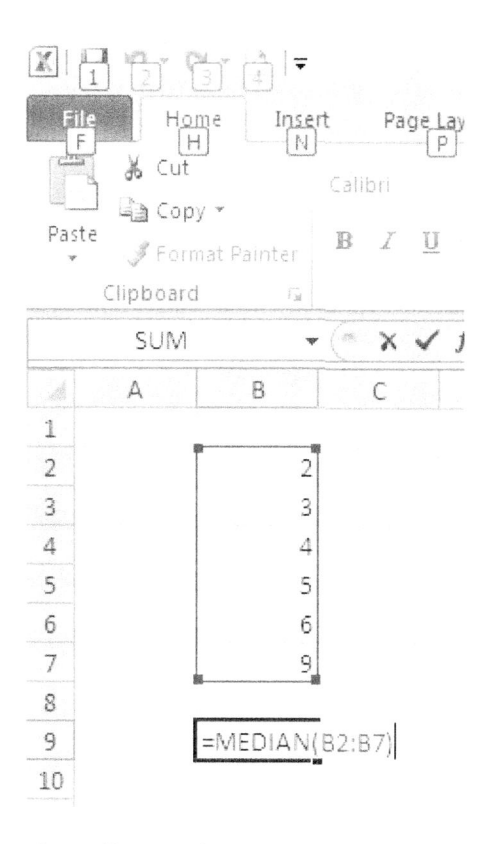

	A	B	C
1			
2		2	
3		3	
4		4	
5		5	
6		6	
7		9	
8			
9		=MEDIAN(B2:B7)	
10			

The Median Function

Ralph V. Celone

CHAPTER 7

Ralph V. Celone

CHAPTER 7
MODE

The Mode is the measurement that appears most frequently in a series of measurements.

0.23540	0.23570	0.23650	0.23520	0.23510
0.23550	0.23570	0.23630	0.23530	0.23580
0.23530	**0.23560**	0.23640	0.23510	0.23530
0.23630	**0.23560**	0.23615	0.23460	0.23540
0.23640	0.23545	0.23660	0.23470	0.23530
0.23670	0.23470	0.23650	0.23440	**0.23560**
0.23490	0.23440	0.23650	0.23590	0.23520
0.23520	0.23450	0.23575	**0.23560**	0.23535
0.23500	0.23670	0.23575	0.23550	0.23540
0.23580	0.23610	0.23580	**0.23560**	**0.23560**

For example, the most common reading in the above data is 0.23560 – that is the Mode. The "mode" function in Excel® will return the Mode of a set of measurements – columns, rows, tables, or isolated numbers – similar to the average and median functions. The syntax of the "mode" function is demonstrated in the next picture.

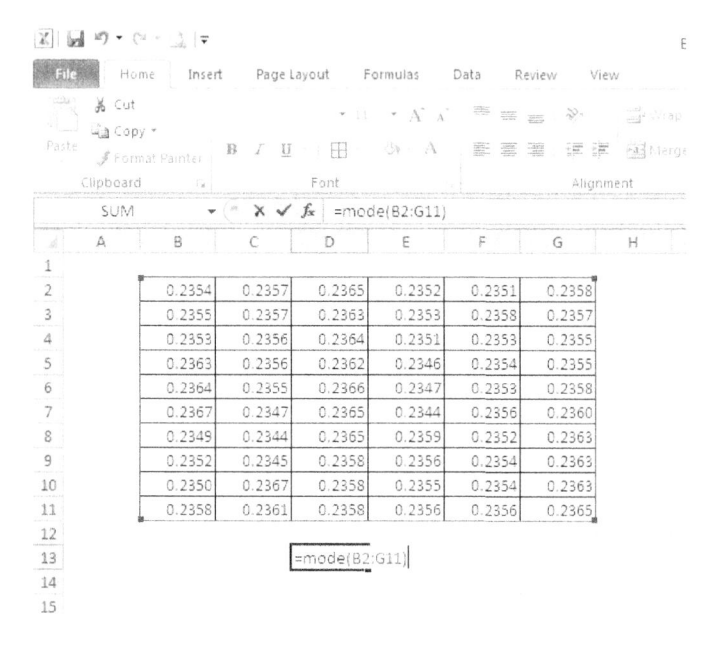

The Mode Function

CHAPTER 8

Ralph V. Celone

CHAPTER 8
RANGE

The Range is the difference between the largest number and the smallest number in a group of measurements or observations. Mathematically, it can be written as *Range=Largest-Smallest*. Let's go back to our M&Ms® and add this data.

Name	Orange	Red	Green	Blue	Yellow	Brown	Total
Frank	17	9	7	18	3	4	58
Al	17	3	9	12	3	7	51
Dave	18	6	8	8	4	8	52
Greg	12	3	10	20	4	6	55
Tom	16	10	7	18	4	1	56
Average	16	6.2	8.2	15.2	3.6	5.2	54.4

Dave had the largest number of orange candies at 18 and Greg had the smallest number of orange candies at 12. So, we can calculate the range for the orange candies as 18 – 12 = 6. If we go through and do the same for the other colors and the total, our updated table would look like this:

Name	Orange	Red	Green	Blue	Yellow	Brown	Total
Frank	17	9	7	18	3	4	58
Al	17	3	9	12	3	7	51
Dave	18	6	8	8	4	8	52
Greg	12	3	10	20	4	6	55
Tom	16	10	7	18	4	1	56
Average	16	6.2	8.2	15.2	3.6	5.2	54.4
Largest	18	10	10	20	4	8	58
Smallest	12	3	7	8	3	1	51
Range	6	7	3	12	1	7	7

For more practice with Range calculations, refer to the accompanying Excel® file called EZ SPC.xlsx and look in the tab called Range.

The Average and the Range are the day-to-day workhorses of any SPC program. Please make sure you thoroughly understand both concepts.

Excel® does not have a function to directly calculate the range of a set of measurements. However, we can use Excel®'s "min" and "max" functions to find the smallest and largest numbers in a group of measurements and subtract the "min" from the "max".

EZ SPC – Statistical Process Control Demystified

	A	B	C	D	E	F	G	H
1								
2		0.2354	0.2357	0.2365	0.2352	0.2351	0.2358	
3		0.2355	0.2357	0.2363	0.2353	0.2358	0.2357	
4		0.2353	0.2356	0.2364	0.2351	0.2353	0.2355	
5		0.2363	0.2356	0.2362	0.2346	0.2354	0.2355	
6		0.2364	0.2355	0.2366	0.2347	0.2353	0.2358	
7		0.2367	0.2347	0.2365	0.2344	0.2356	0.2360	
8		0.2349	0.2344	0.2365	0.2359	0.2352	0.2363	
9		0.2352	0.2345	0.2358	0.2356	0.2354	0.2363	
10		0.2350	0.2367	0.2358	0.2355	0.2354	0.2363	
11		0.2358	0.2361	0.2358	0.2356	0.2356	0.2365	
12								
13				Range	=max(B2:G11)-min(B2:G11)			

Formula bar: `=max(B2:G11)-min(B2:G11)`

Synthesizing a Range Function

Ralph V. Celone

CHAPTER 9

Ralph V. Celone

CHAPTER 9
HISTOGRAMS

Histograms are frequency plots. They tell you how frequently a measurement has been recorded. They are a graphical display of how your process has performed. A histogram of the call center response times discussed earlier is shown below.

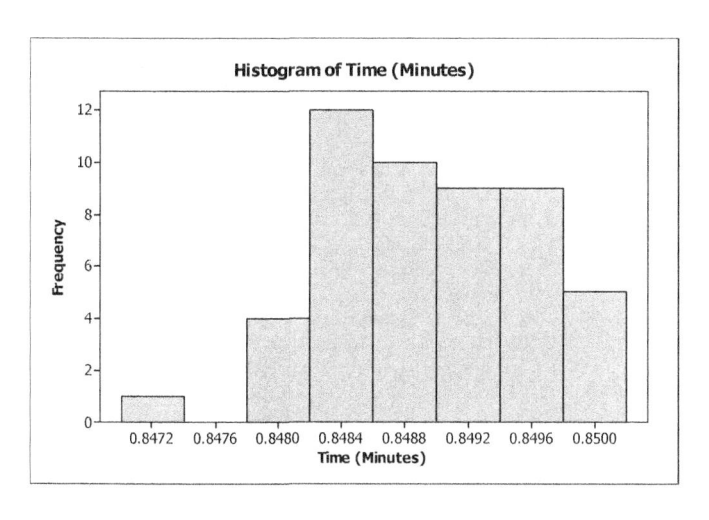

Excel® has some inherent ability to generate rudimentary Histograms if you enable the Analysis ToolPak. There are many other software packages, such as Minitab®, and other third party add-ins for Excel® that can generate better looking histograms using your process data.

However, to better understand the mechanics of creating a histogram, work through an example using the 30 measurements in the following table.

Sample	Meas A
1	13
2	14
3	14
4	11
5	11
6	10
7	9
8	10
9	11
10	10

Sample	Meas A
11	11
12	13
13	8
14	13
15	12
16	11
17	12
18	10
19	12
20	11

Sample	Meas A
21	12
22	12
23	9
24	13
25	11
26	11
27	11
28	9
29	10
30	14

A quick look through the data reveals that the smallest measurement is 8 and the largest is 14. Based on that range, construct a grid similar to the one below.

Measurement A

10								
9								
8								
7								
6								
5								
4								
3								
2								
1								
	7	8	9	10	11	12	13	14	15

Then go through the list of measurements and fill in a block above each corresponding number – the first four measurements should look like this:

Measurement A

10								
9								
8								
7								
6								
5								
4								
3								
2						▓		
1				▓		▓		
	7	8	9	10	11	12	13	14	15

Go through all the data and plot all 30 measurements. The final histogram should be very similar to the one shown below.

Measurement A

10								
9					▓			
8					▓			
7					▓			
6					▓			
5				▓	▓			
4				▓	▓	▓		
3				▓	▓	▓	▓	
2			▓	▓	▓	▓	▓	
1		▓	▓	▓	▓	▓	▓	
	7	8	9	10	11	12	13	14	15

For more practice with Histograms, refer to the accompanying Excel® file called EZ SPC.xlsx and look in the tab called Histogram.

The pattern the measurements create on a Histogram is called a Distribution of the measurements. There are various types of distributions: Gaussian, Poisson, and Random to name just a few. Each type of distribution has its own properties. For example, a Gaussian distribution (also called a Normal distribution) will appear as a bell-shaped curve. A Poisson distribution is not symmetrical about its Mean value and its Variance is equal to its Mean. What people most commonly work with is the bell-shaped curve that is called the Gaussian, or Normal distribution. There is a theorem in mathematics (which is beyond the scope of this book) called the Central Limit Theorem that allows us to work with various types of distributions as if they were Normal distributions. Going forward we will work with all distributions as if they were Normal distributions.

Histograms can help to visualize what is actually happening in a process. The following graphic is an Excel® generated histogram showing the distribution of patient ages at a healthcare facility. We can see that we have peaks near 52, 69, and, to a lesser extent, 31 years of age. Someone from the insurance industry who saw this data might want to do further research to understand why those particular age groups stand out and are more likely to show up as patients at the facility.

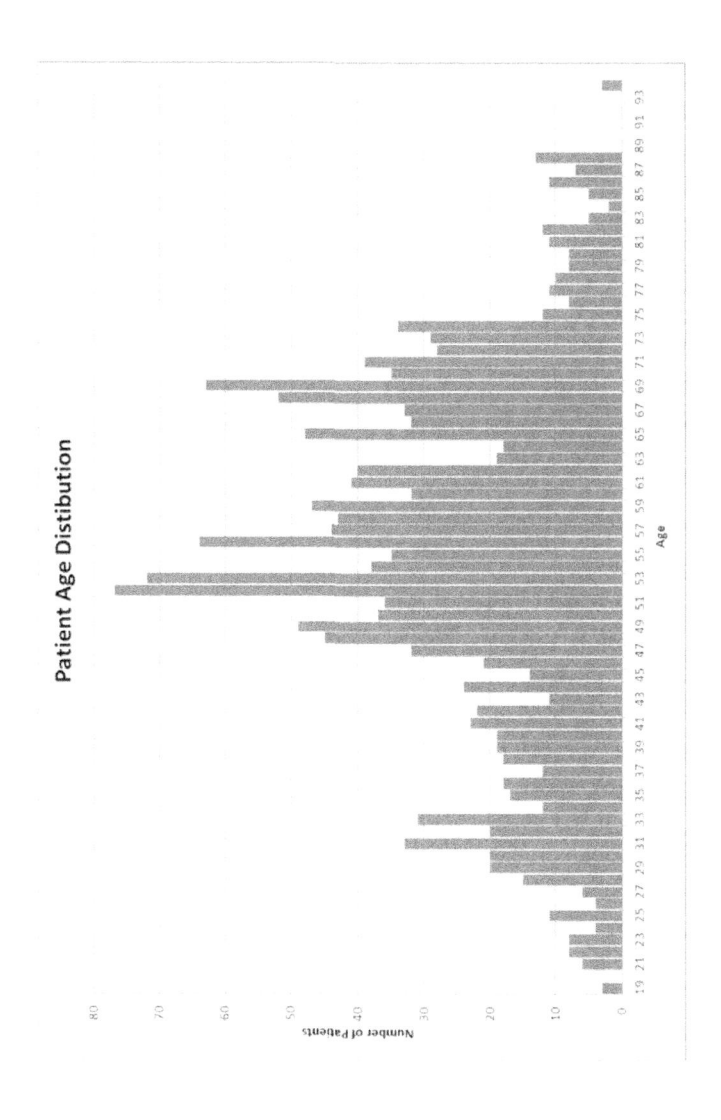

Patient Age Distribution

CHAPTER 10

Ralph V. Celone

CHAPTER 10
STANDARD DEVIATION

Standard Deviation is a measure of how much the process varies relative to the Mean. The calculation is based on the "spread" of measurements around the Mean. It is an indication of process variation. The smaller the Standard Deviation, the smaller the variation in the process. In general, smaller Standard Deviations are preferred over larger Standard Deviations. When analyzed graphically, "skinnier" is usually better. The following two histograms were created from a process before and after process improvements were made. All of the plotting parameters are identical between histograms. Run2 has a much smaller Standard Deviation and much sharper peak than Run1, meaning Run2 is much more predictable.

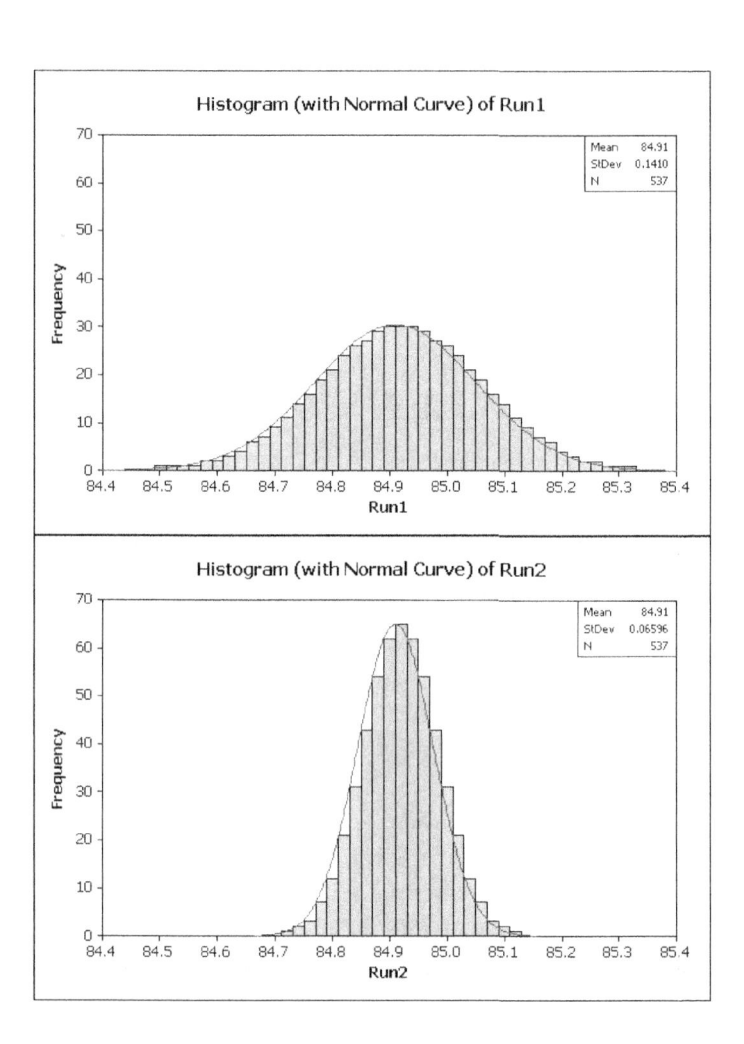

Histogram (with Normal Curve) of Run1

Mean 84.91
StDev 0.1410
N 537

Histogram (with Normal Curve) of Run2

Mean 84.91
StDev 0.06596
N 537

The symbol for Standard Deviation is the Greek letter sigma (σ).

The Standard Deviation can be calculated using fairly straightforward math. The calculations are detailed on the following pages. However, the process is quite tedious and laborious. It is much simpler to use a calculator with statistical functions, Excel®, or any other of the various statistical software packages available. The Excel® function "stdev" will return the Standard Deviation of a group of measurements.

Consider a set of 10 measurements (2, 2, 4, 4, 4, 5, 5, 6, 7, 9). To calculate the Standard Deviation, the first step is to calculate the Mean: 2 + 2 + 4 + 4 + 4 + 5 + 5 + 6 + 7 + 9 = 48 and 48 divided by 10 equals 4.8, so our Mean is 4.8.

Step two is to calculate the squared difference between each measurement and the Mean as follows:

$$(2 - 4.8)^2 = 7.84$$
$$(2 - 4.8)^2 = 7.84$$
$$(4 - 4.8)^2 = 0.64$$
$$(4 - 4.8)^2 = 0.64$$
$$(4 - 4.8)^2 = 0.64$$
$$(5 - 4.8)^2 = 0.04$$
$$(5 - 4.8)^2 = 0.04$$
$$(6 - 4.8)^2 = 1.44$$
$$(7 - 4.8)^2 = 4.84$$
$$\underline{(9 - 4.8)^2 = 17.64}$$
$$41.6$$

Step three is to take the sum of all those squared differences (41.6) and divide by the number of measurements minus one (n-1):

$41.6 \div 9 = 4.6222$ (this is called the Variance)

Step four is to finally calculate the Standard Deviation by taking the square root of the Variance:

$\sqrt{4.6222} = 2.1499 = Standard\ Deviation = \sigma$

It is important to understand Standard Deviation because it is used to calculate the Control Limits that we will discuss in a few more pages.

The next two figures illustrate some important properties related to Standard Deviation.

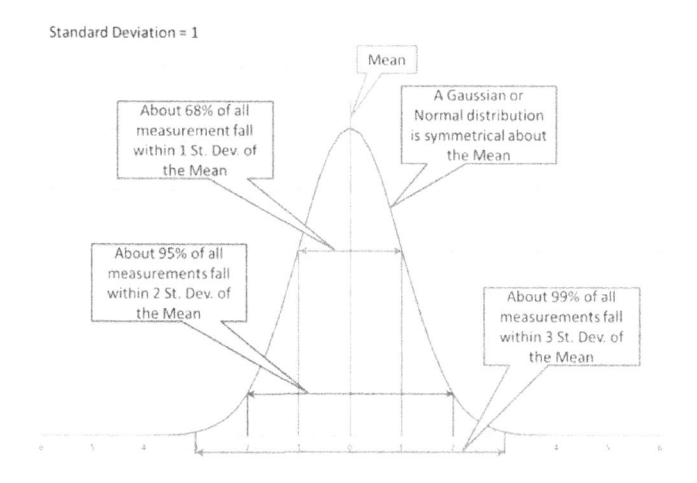

![Standard Deviation = 1 normal distribution diagram showing Mean at center, about 68% of all measurements fall within 1 St. Dev. of the Mean, about 95% within 2 St. Dev., about 99% within 3 St. Dev., and noting that a Gaussian or Normal distribution is symmetrical about the Mean]

Note that about 68% of the points lie within one Standard Deviation of the Mean, about 95% of the points lie within two standard deviations of the Mean, and, about 99.8% of the distribution lies within three standard deviations of the Mean.

![Mean = 0 chart comparing three normal distributions with St Dev = 0.5, St Dev = 1, and St Dev = 2, across x-axis from -6 to 6]

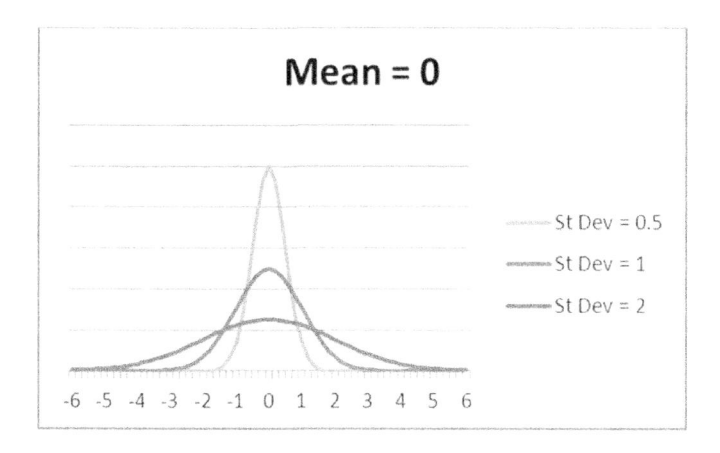

Note that as the Standard Deviation increases, the distribution becomes less sharp and flattens out –

meaning the measurements are spread over a wider range and the process being measured has more variability.

For more practice with Standard Deviation calculations, refer to the accompanying Excel® file called EZ SPC.xlsx and look in the tab called St. Dev.

Excel® also has a function named "stdev" that will calculate the Standard Deviation as shown in the following picture.

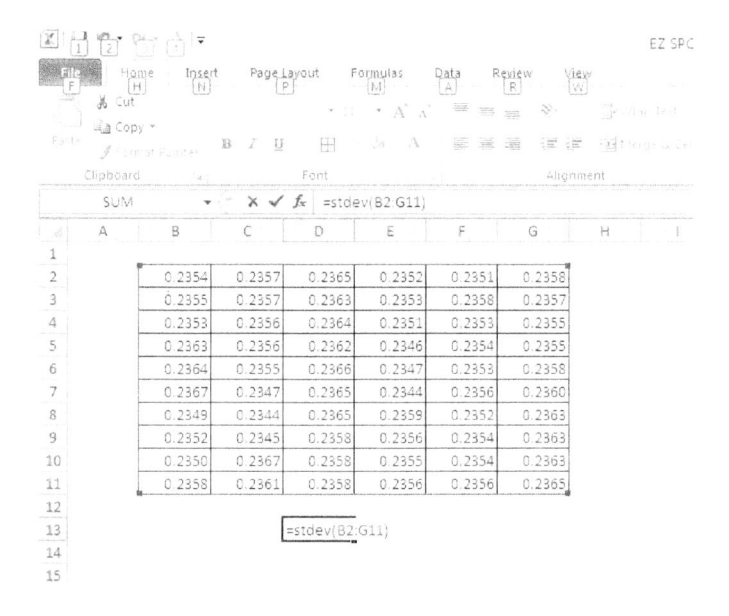

Syntax of Standard Deviation Function

CHAPTER 11

CHAPTER 11
SPECIFICATION LIMITS

Specification Limits or Spec. Limits are the definition of acceptable outputs of a process as set forth by the customer. They consist of a Lower Spec. Limit (LSL) and an Upper Spec. Limit (USL). These specifications can be written in a couple of different ways. For example, suppose we have a machined part that must have a diameter of at least 0.8347 inches, but no more than 0.8582 inches. In this case the LSL is 0.8347 inches and USL is 0.8582 inches. This could also be written as 0.84645 ± 0.01175 inches (this would be spoken as 0.84645 plus or minus 0.01175 inches).

Here are some additional examples of Spec. Limits:

Cardiac-specific troponins I and T (cTnI and cTnT) are troponins that are found only in the heart and normally only in minute or undetectable quantities. When the heart muscle is damaged, these proteins are released into the bloodstream in amounts that are proportional to the amount of damage to the heart. An Emergency Room doctor will typically order a blood test to check for these cardiac-specific proteins if he or she suspects that you are having a heart attack. Given the seriousness of this condition, most hospitals have put specification limits on the turnaround time for these lab tests. They typically require a turnaround time of 60 minutes or less. In this case, the LSL is zero and the USL is 60 minutes.

I worked at one particular manufacturer where certain customers had strict inventory control requirements and specified the ship date on the parts they required. We were allowed to ship up to five days early or up to five days after the customer's stated ship date without upsetting the customer. Therefore, the LSL was (ship date minus 5 days) and the USL was (ship date plus 5 days).

Steel is a commodity that is sold by the pound. In a business that uses huge amounts of steel and has a relationship with the steel mills, a smart materials manager will ask the mill to "roll it on the thin side" so that he can buy more surface area of steel for the same amount of money. Here are the numbers: 10 gauge steel has a nominal thickness of 0.1345 inches with a USL of 0.1405 inches and an LSL of 0.1285 inches (or 0.1345 ± 0.0060 inches). Rolling on the thin side will change the USL to 0.1345 and keep the LSL at 0.1285 (now we're at 0.1315 ± 0.003) – still within the overall spec. for 10 gauge steel but the buying company will get more square feet per pound and save money.

CHAPTER 12

Ralph V. Celone

CHAPTER 12
CONTROL LIMITS

Unlike Spec. Limits, Control Limits are calculated directly from measurements taken from the process itself and have nothing to do with the Spec. Limits (LSL & USL). There is a Lower Control Limit (LCL) and an Upper Control Limit (UCL). Ideally, the LCL and UCL lie between the LSL and USL and the process will produce acceptable results. However, I have seen manufacturing processes where one or the other (or both) of the Control Limits fell outside of the Spec. Limits. That is a condition that guarantees that the process will produce unacceptable results.

The Control Limits are generally set at plus and minus three Standard Deviations from the process Mean (Mean $\pm$ 3σ). So to calculate the control limits, you must be able to calculate the Mean and the Standard Deviation of your process. You must also perform the calculations with enough (generally a minimum of

30) observations to insure that you have a large enough sample size to give you an accurate representation of the process.

The 30 observations should be taken as random samples as part of a larger run. Let's take 30 measurements from our Call Center data. They are:

Obs	Minutes	Obs	Minutes	Obs	Minutes
1	0.84925	11	0.84860	21	0.84940
2	0.84925	12	0.84795	22	0.84995
3	0.84930	13	0.84815	23	0.84945
4	0.84890	14	0.84850	24	0.84975
5	0.84875	15	0.84855	25	0.84975
6	0.84875	16	0.84915	26	0.85010
7	0.84820	17	0.84875	27	0.85000
8	0.84845	18	0.84910	28	0.84965
9	0.84835	19	0.84945	29	0.84970
10	0.84825	20	0.84935	30	0.84965

Our Mean is 0.84908 and our Standard Deviation is 0.000612. Three Standard Deviations (3σ) are equal to 0.001836. So, our LCL = 0.84908 − 0.001836 = 0.84724 and our UCL = 0.84908 + 0.001836 = 0.85092.

We put the LCL and UCL calculations into equations as follows:

$$LCL = \mu - 3\sigma \text{ and } UCL = \mu + 3\sigma$$

CHAPTER 13

Ralph V. Celone

CHAPTER 13
SAMPLING

Sampling is how often the output of the process is to be measured and recorded. Sampling is a very important consideration and will be almost entirely dictated by the process output.

In a process that is run on an automated machine that is producing hundreds or thousands of pieces per hour, the sampling requirement might be five pieces per hour or five pieces every 30 minutes. These should be random pieces taken directly from the machine output.

In a small, community-based hospital the cardiac-specific troponins test time may include every test performed in a shift or in a day because of the small quantity of patients presenting with symptoms requiring this type of testing.

If you sample too often, you will sacrifice efficiency in your labor costs. If you sample too infrequently, you may miss capturing early indications of a process trending toward an out-of-spec. condition.

In most cases, you need to balance the cost required to perform and document the process measurements against the risk of not detecting a defect from the process.

CHAPTER 14

CHAPTER 14
CONTROL CHARTS

We now have enough knowledge and tools to begin to create a Control Chart. Control Charts are used to graphically display the process data that is being measured. The next two figures are examples of the top and bottom sections of a blank Control Chart. A Control Chart template is included in the EZ SPC.xlsx file. It is designed to be printed on 11"x17" paper. It is set up to be as generic as possible and not every item in the header will apply to every process. The next few pages will discuss each item on the template.

Ralph V. Celone

EZ SPC – Statistical Process Control Demystified

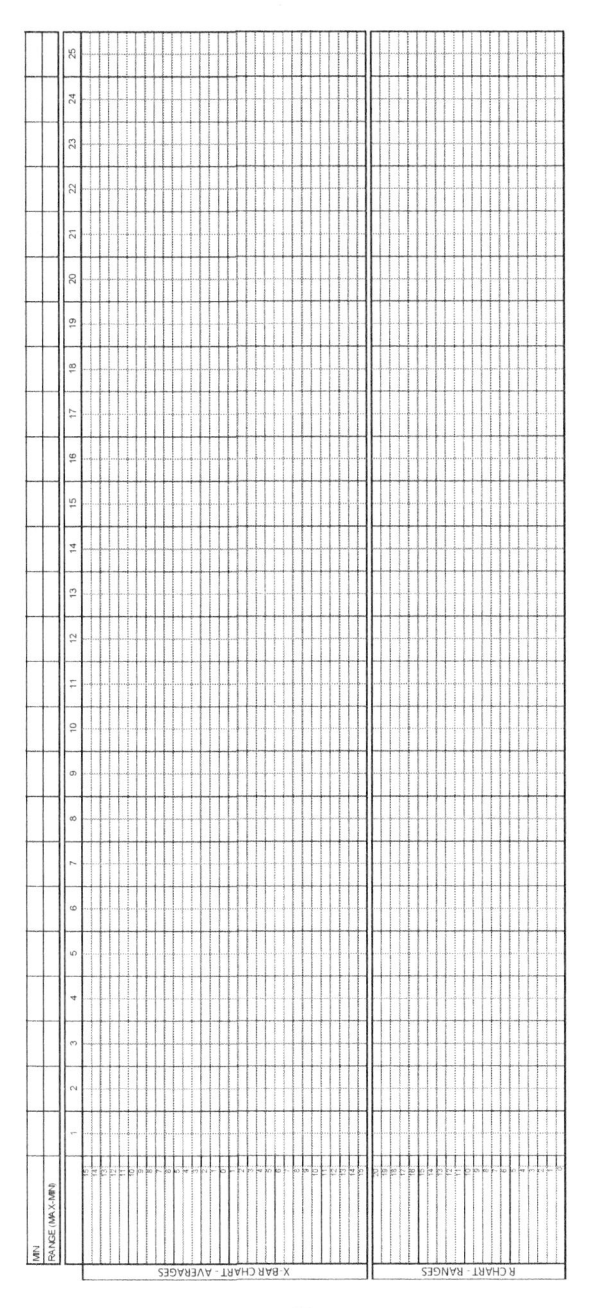

Header Items

Your company logo here

Customer	Operation
Part No.	Business Unit
Parameter	Machine

Specification	Chart No.
Gage	Unit of Measure
Sample Size/Frequency	Zero Equals

The first field on the template is an area reserved for your company logo. While not required, this enhances the professional appearance. The next twelve fields are background data to help identify the process.

Customer – used to capture the customer name or number when a process is being performed for a specific customer.

Part No. – used to capture identification information when the process is being performed on a specific part.

Parameter – used to capture exactly what is being measured. For example, overall length, queuing time, temperature, etc.

Operation – used to record the name of the particular operation being performed. For example, grinding, order entry, heat treating, etc.

Business Unit – used to record business unit name or number.

Machine – used to record machine name or number when the process is associated with a specific machine or production line.

Specification – used to record the acceptable performance limits of the process. For example, 1,100 ± 50 degrees F, less than 25 seconds, etc.

Gage – used to record the name or number of the particular measuring instrument used to make the measurement.

Sample Size/Frequency – used to record the sampling requirement.

Chart No. – used to keep track of charts and keep them in order.

Unit of Measure – used to record the units of measure used in the process. For example, inches, millimeters, seconds, degrees F or degrees C, etc.

Zero Equals – used to record the Zero point on the X-Bar Chart and is a calculated number that is roughly equal to the process Mean.

Calculation Area Items

Date				
Time				
Lot No.				
Operator				
Measurement 1				
Measurement 2				
Measurement 3				
Measurement 4				
Measurement 5				
Sum				
Average (X-Bar)				
MAX				
MIN				
RANGE (MAX-MIN)				

This area is used to record all of the numerical process measurements and consists of the following fields:

Date – used to record the date of when the process was sampled and its output measured.

Time – used to record the time when the process was sampled and its output measured.

Lot No. – this field is useful in manufacturing situations to record the lot number of raw material or a run number, but can be used to capture any other data as required.

Operator – used to record the name or number of the person running the process and taking the measurements.

Measurement 1 to 5 – each time a process is sampled, these fields are used to record the raw measurements.

Sum – is the sum of the five measurements.

Average – is the Average or Mean of the five measurements.

MAX – is the largest of the five measurements.

MIN – is the smallest of the five measurements.

RANGE (MAX-MIN) – is the MAX minus the MIN.

Below is an example of how this might look with some of our call center data:

Date	1/23	1/23		
Time	0800	0815		
Lot No.	—	—		
Operator	RVC	RVC		
Measurement 1	.84925	.84875		
Measurement 2	.84925	.84820		
Measurement 3	.84930	.84845		
Measurement 4	.84890	.84835		
Measurement 5	.84875	.84825		
Sum	4.2455	4.242		
Average (X-Bar)	.84909	.8484		
MAX	.84930	.84875		
MIN	.84875	.8482		
RANGE (MAX-MIN)	.00055	.00055		

The Average (X-Bar) row gets plotted on the X-Bar chart.

The RANGE (MAX-MIN) row gets plotted on the R chart.

Charting Area

This area is where the actual charting takes place and has two main areas. One area is for charting the Average, Mean, or, X-Bar of the five samples taken from the process and one area is for charting the Range of the five samples.

These two areas are shown on the next page. Note that in the X-Bar or Average area, the center of the chart is zero and there are gradations both above and below the zero point. This is because we graph our process Mean along the zero point and sample averages may be more or less than the process Mean.

The X-Bar or Average area is also where we will plot our Upper and Lower Control Limits along with our Upper and Lower Specification Limits.

The Range area contains only numbers above the zero point because the calculation for Range always yields a positive number.

Both areas should be scaled to fit the particular process that is being studied.

Let's use the call center data to illustrate how these two areas are plotted. We have been given the LSL and USL as 0.83470 and 0.85820, respectively. From a large sample of the process data, we have calculated the following parameters:

Average	0.85000		UCL	0.85600
St Dev	0.00200		LCL	0.84400

X-BAR CHART - AVERAGES

USL 0.8582
UCL 0.8560
0.85
LCL 0.8440
LSL 0.8347

R CHART - RANGES

0.0007
0.0006
0.0005
0.0004
0.0003
0.0002
0.0001

Looking at the control chart, we can see that our process is not exactly centered between our LSL and USL. This may indicate a problem with the process design or it may be intentional. I have worked at factories that would purposely form metal parts towards one end or the other of the specification range to account for deformation of the part during subsequent heat treating or other processes.

We can also see that the process Mean is centered between the LCL and UCL. Since the LCL and UCL are calculated using the process Mean $\pm\ 3\sigma$, the Mean should always be centered between the LCL and UCL. If it's not, go back and double check your calculations.

The next page shows a more complete X-Bar/R Chart.

	1	2	3	4	5	6	7	8	9	10	11	12	13	14	15	16	17	18
Measurement 1	0.84925	0.84875	0.84860	0.84915	0.84940	0.85010	0.84995	0.84825	0.84710	0.84850	0.84960	0.84960	0.84945	0.85050	0.84865	0.85000	0.85060	0.85045
Measurement 2	0.84925	0.84820	0.84795	0.84875	0.84995	0.85000	0.84990	0.84920	0.84815	0.84880	0.84950	0.85015	0.84960	0.85055	0.84935	0.84995	0.85020	0.85100
Measurement 3	0.84930	0.84845	0.84815	0.84910	0.84945	0.84965	0.84975	0.84900	0.84880	0.84870	0.84945	0.84990	0.85030	0.85045	0.84980	0.85000	0.84960	0.85075
Measurement 4	0.84890	0.84835	0.84850	0.84945	0.84975	0.84970	0.84815	0.84925	0.84875	0.84856	0.84955	0.84995	0.85020	0.84915	0.84965	0.85020	0.84970	0.85000
Measurement 5	0.84875	0.84825	0.84855	0.84935	0.84975	0.84965	0.84825	0.84830	0.84860	0.84850	0.84935	0.84960	0.85020	0.84935	0.84950	0.85045	0.84980	0.85025
Sum	4.24545	4.24200	4.24175	4.24580	4.24830	4.24910	4.24600	4.24400	4.24140	4.24305	4.24745	4.24940	4.24975	4.25000	4.24715	4.25060	4.24990	4.25245
Average (X-Bar)	0.84909	0.84840	0.84835	0.84918	0.84966	0.84982	0.84920	0.84880	0.84828	0.84861	0.84949	0.84988	0.84995	0.85000	0.84943	0.85012	0.84998	0.85049
MAX	0.84930	0.84875	0.84860	0.84945	0.84995	0.85010	0.84995	0.84925	0.84880	0.84880	0.84960	0.85015	0.85030	0.85055	0.84985	0.85045	0.85060	0.85100
MIN	0.84875	0.84820	0.84795	0.84875	0.84940	0.84965	0.84815	0.84825	0.84710	0.84850	0.84935	0.84960	0.84945	0.84915	0.84865	0.84995	0.84960	0.85000
RANGE (MAX-MIN)	0.00055	0.00055	0.00065	0.00070	0.00055	0.00045	0.00180	0.00100	0.00170	0.00030	0.00025	0.00055	0.00085	0.00140	0.00120	0.00050	0.00100	0.00100

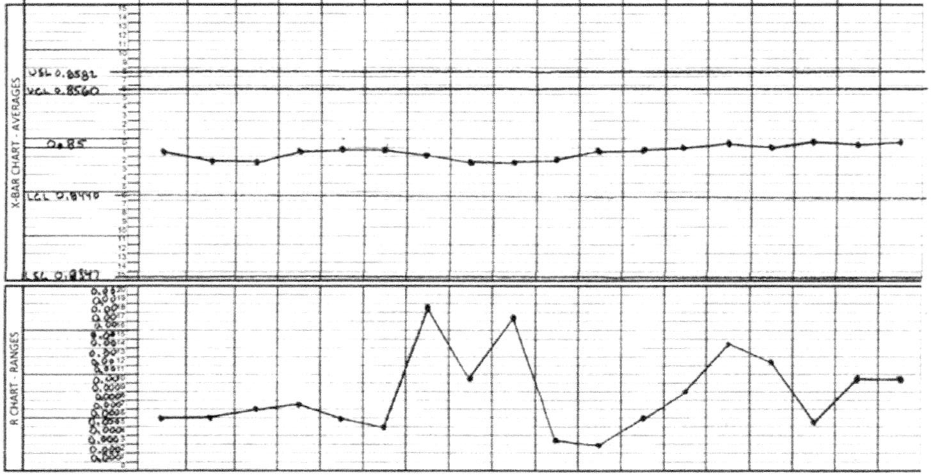

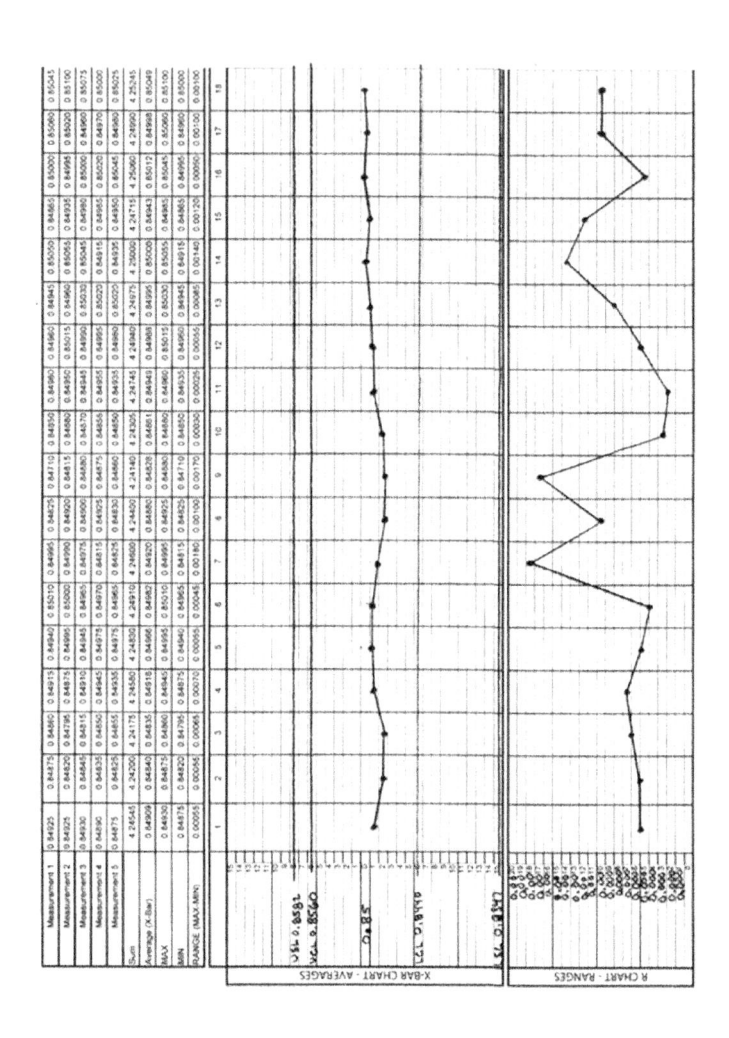

Trouble Indicators

X-Bar/R Charts are a great way to graphically display process performance. If we know what to look for, we can use these tools to know at a glance if we need to intervene in the process.

All processes have some natural (or random) variation in their output. We will use the X-Bar/R Chart to identify when this variation is no longer random and is beginning to form trends.

Of course if any single point is outside of the Control Limits or is outside of the Specification Limits, it should be obvious that immediate action must be taken. The process, or measurement system, may have suffered a sudden, catastrophic failure. However, it is also important to note that any particular process may be performing within the Specification Limits – it may even be performing within the Control Limits – but may still need some type of investigation because it has developed a trend. Remember our SPC goal is to predict trouble <u>before</u> it occurs.

For our purposes, a trend will have at least one of the following characteristics:

- A. seven consecutive points on one side of the Average
- B. seven consecutive points consistently increasing
- C. seven consecutive points consistently decreasing
- D. cycling – even within the Control Limits.

Any one of these characteristics is indicative of a problem. It may be a problem with the process or it may be a problem with the measurement system. Either way, the root cause needs to be determined and the appropriate corrective action taken.

The next few pages will discuss trending characteristics.

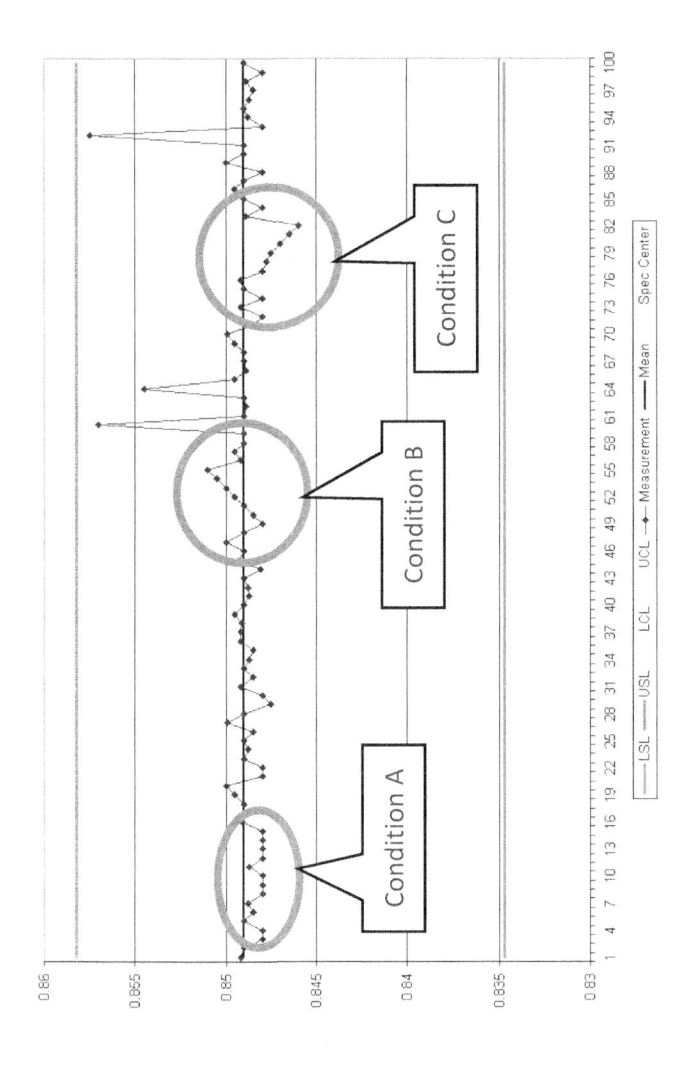

EZ SPC – Statistical Process Control Demystified

93

Condition A – Seven consecutive points on one side of the Average. This condition may not seem to be an obvious trend, but, the process should vary randomly about the Mean. Seven points on the same side of the Mean have taken enough of the randomness out of the process to warrant further investigation.

Condition B – Seven consecutive points consistently increasing. This indicates a trend and shows that the process is drifting towards its upper limits and is showing a definite pattern rather than random variation about the Mean.

Condition C – Seven consecutive points consistently decreasing. Again, this indicates a trend and shows that the process is showing a definite pattern rather than random variation about the Mean. In this case the process is showing a definite drift towards its lower limits.

Condition D – The next page shows a special type of trend called "cycling". This particular trend shows a sinusoidal shape. However, any repetitive pattern is an indicator of cycling in the process. The patterns may be square, triangular or any other shape, but if they are repetitive, then the process is cycling.

Cycling may or may not be acceptable in your particular process. If you were to measure the temperature in most homes, you would find that it cycled in a repetitive manner as the contacts in the thermostat opened and closed.

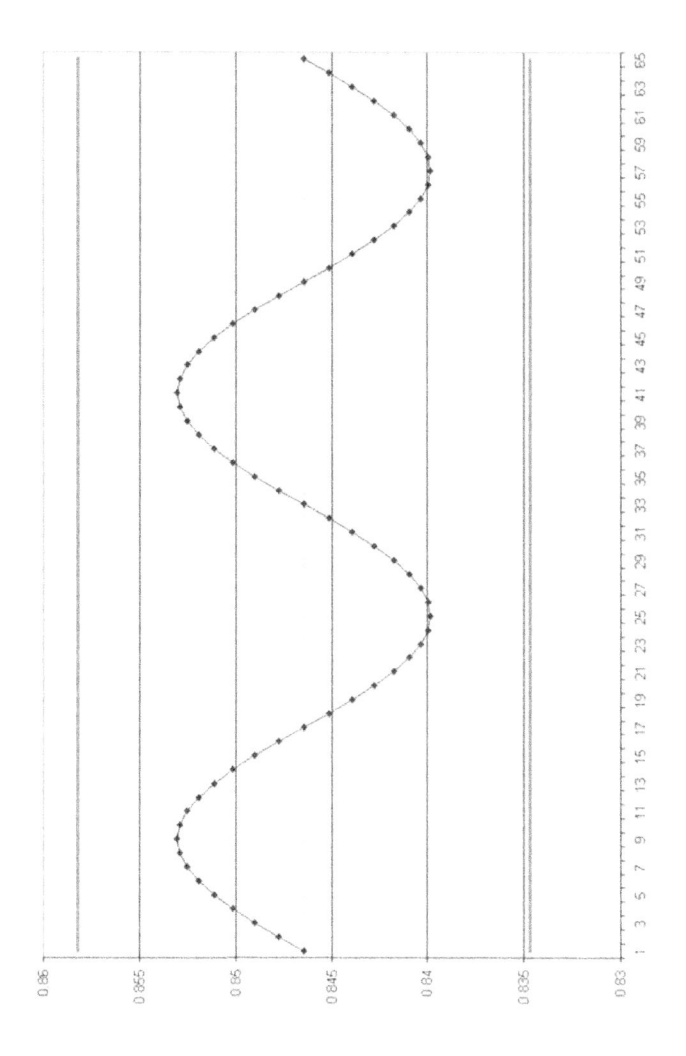

Cycling may occur along various timelines. Most consumer grade ovens will cycle over a period of a few tens of minutes. I once worked in a facility that implemented a new automated inspection system that used cameras to perform an automated optical inspection of finished parts. The inspection system worked great on the First and Third shifts, but started producing erroneous results about an hour into the Second shift for about an hour each day. To make a long story short, at that time each day the sun shone through a particular window onto the machine disturbing the background lighting for the cameras and generating erroneous results. The period of cycling in this instance was about 24 hours.

If cycling, whether or not it remains within the control limits, cannot be tolerated in your process, then the root cause of the cycling must be determined and eliminated.

It is important to remember that the X-Bar part of the chart is a series of averages and that a point above the USL and a point below the LSL could average out to the center of the Specification Limits. Therefore, we cannot rely solely on averages to tell the entire story and must use some additional indicators to help warn us of impending trouble.

One additional trouble indicator can be taken from the Range area of the SPC chart. If the Range is increasing, that is an indication that the variation in the process is increasing and the process is heading for an unstable condition.

CHAPTER 15

CHAPTER 15
PROCESS PERFORMANCE

Once SPC data is being gathered and plotted, the next logical step is to use that data in a Process Improvement program. Since you can't change what you can't measure, you need some way to quantify Process Performance (Pp). There is a set of equations to calculate Process Performance (Pp) and the Process Performance Index (Ppk). Pp and Ppk are usually used to validate process improvements. Larger values for Pp and Ppk indicate better Process Performance. The calculation for Pp is based on the Specification Limits and Standard Deviation of the process as shown on the next page.

$$Pp = \frac{(USL - LSL)}{6\sigma}$$

Where:
USL is the Upper Specification Limit
LSL is the Lower Specification Limit
σ is the process Standard Deviation

Note that this equation is only an indication of how wide the Specification Limits are relative to the process Standard Deviation. This equation does not tell the entire story. It could be possible to have a process running with a very tight Standard Deviation with every measurement outside of the Specification Limits and this equation would provide a high value for Pp even though every output of the process was a defect. To take that possibility into account, we calculate the Process Performance Index (Ppk). The procedure essentially splits the Pp equation in two along the process Mean. The first part of the split gives an Upper Process Performance (PPU) between the Upper Spec. Limit and the Mean. The second part of the split gives a Lower Process Performance (PPL) between the Mean and the Lower Spec. Limit. These dual equations can yield a more complete measure of how a process is performing. The Process Performance Index (Ppk) is the lesser of the two calculations.

You can think of the Process Performance (Pp) measurement as determining whether a car will fit in a garage and the Process Performance Index (Ppk) as how well the car is centered in the garage.

The equations for PPL, PPU, and Ppk are shown below.

$$Ppk = min\ [PPU, PPL]$$

$$PPU = \frac{(USL - \mu)}{3\sigma}\ and\ PPL = \frac{(\mu - LSL)}{3\sigma}$$

$$Ppk = min\ \left[\frac{(USL - \mu)}{3\sigma}, \frac{(\mu - LSL)}{3\sigma}\right]$$

Where:
USL is the Upper Specification Limit
LSL is the Lower Specification Limit
μ is the process Mean
σ is the process Standard Deviation

When calculating Ppk, we calculate the two intermediate quantities of PPL and PPU and then take the smaller of the two values as the Ppk. While Pp is a single calculation, Ppk is the smaller of the two separate calculations.

$$PPU = \frac{(USL - \mu)}{3\sigma}\ and\ PPL = \frac{(\mu - LSL)}{3\sigma}$$

In theory, the Mean and Standard Deviation should be calculated using measurements of each individual output (the entire population) of the process. However, in practice this is not always feasible and the calculations are based on as large a sample size as practical.

One of the major goals of any Process Improvement program is to reduce the variation in the process. Note that the bottom (denominator) of each equation for Pp and Ppk contains a term for the Standard Deviation of the process. This means as the variation in the process is reduced (which will reduce the Standard Deviation), Pp and Ppk will increase. Also note that the calculations for Ppk take into account the Mean value of the process. This means that if the process Mean is beyond one of the Specification Limits, Ppk can take on negative values. This is not a desirable condition and must be corrected by changing the process such that the average value of measurements moves toward the center of the Specification Limits. This has given rise to the term "Shift the Mean".

We can use our Call Center data to illustrate the Pp and Ppk calculations. If our LSL is defined as 0.83470 and our USL is defined as 0.85820 and from a large sample of the process data, we have calculated that the Average (or Mean) is 0.85000 and the Standard Deviation is 0.00200. Process Performance is calculated as follows:

$$Pp = \frac{(USL - LSL)}{6\sigma}$$

$$Pp = \frac{(0.85820 - 0.83470)}{6(0.00200)}$$

$$Pp = 1.958$$

The Process Performance Index (Ppk) is calculated below:

$$Ppk = min\left[\frac{(USL - \mu)}{3\sigma}, \frac{(\mu - LSL)}{3\sigma}\right]$$

$$Ppk = \min[PPU, PPL]$$

$$Ppk = min\frac{(0.8582 - 0.8500)}{3(0.0020)}, \frac{(0.8500 - 0.8347)}{3(0.0020)}$$

$$Ppk = min\ [1.367, 2.550]$$

$$Ppk = 1.367$$

These are fairly straightforward calculations but there is a template in the Ppk tab of the Excel® file if you would like to double-check your calculations.

Ralph V. Celone

CHAPTER 16

Ralph V. Celone

CHAPTER 16
PROCESS CAPABILITY

There is also a set of equations to calculate Process Capability (Cp) and the Process Capability Index (Cpk). The Process Capability Index (Cpk) is used to predict future performance of a process based on historical data. Cpk predicts the probability of how well your process will meet customer requirements. In fact, your customer may have dictated specific Cpk requirements to you. Like Pp and Ppk, larger values for Cp and Cpk indicate better Process Capability.

It is common for customers to request that you report the Cpk of your processes. In most cases they will specify 1.33 as a minimum value for an existing process or sometimes 1.67 for a measurement that is safety related or is a Critical To Quality (CTQ) measurement.

The calculations for Cpk are very similar to those for Ppk and many people confuse them. The difference between the Cpk and Ppk calculations lies in the method used to calculate the Standard Deviation. While Ppk is calculated using a Standard Deviation that is derived using the square root of the Variance method introduced earlier in this book, Cpk uses an estimate of the Standard Deviation based on the Range of the measurements and what are called "Unbiasing Constants". The Standard Deviation used in the Cpk calculations is written as σ_ω to distinguish it from the Standard Deviation that is calculated using the square root of the Variance discussed earlier.

While it is possible to calculate the Unbiasing Constants based on subgroup size (the number of measurements taken in each sample), that is rarely done in reality. When performing these calculations manually, the constants can be found in other reference books on statistics. A short list of Unbiasing Constants follows.

N	c_4	c_5	d_2	d_3	d_4
1	*	*	1	0.82	1
2	0.797885	0.603	1.128	0.8525	0.954
3	0.886227	0.463	1.693	0.8884	1.588
4	0.921318	0.389	2.059	0.8794	1.978
5	0.939986	0.341	2.326	0.8641	2.257
6	0.951533	0.308	2.534	0.848	2.472
7	0.959369	0.282	2.704	0.8332	2.645
8	0.96503	0.262	2.847	0.8198	2.791
9	0.969311	0.246	2.97	0.8078	2.915
10	0.972659	0.232	3.078	0.7971	3.024
11	0.97535	0.22	3.173	0.7873	3.121
12	0.977559	0.21	3.258	0.7785	3.207
13	0.979406	0.202	3.336	0.7704	3.285
14	0.980971	0.194	3.407	0.763	3.356
15	0.982316	0.187	3.472	0.7562	3.422
16	0.983484	0.181	3.532	0.7499	3.482
17	0.984506	0.175	3.588	0.7441	3.538
18	0.98541	0.17	3.64	0.7386	3.591
19	0.986214	0.166	3.689	0.7335	3.64
20	0.986934	0.161	3.735	0.7287	3.686
21	0.987583	0.157	3.778	0.7242	3.73
22	0.98817	0.153	3.819	0.7199	3.771
23	0.988705	0.15	3.858	0.7159	3.811
24	0.989193	0.147	3.895	0.7121	3.847
25	0.98964	0.144	3.931	0.7084	3.883

Select Unbiasing Constants

I do not recommend the manual calculation of Cpk. With the proliferation and low cost of statistical analysis software packages or add-ins for Excel®, it does not make sense to waste the time it would take for manual calculations. The manual calculations are included here only for completeness and to illustrate the difference from the Ppk calculations.

$$CP = \frac{(USL - LSL)}{6\sigma_\omega}$$

and

$$Cpk = min[CPU, CPL]$$

where

$$CPU = \frac{(USL - \mu)}{3\sigma_\omega} \text{ and } CPL = \frac{(\mu - LSL)}{3\sigma_\omega}$$

Where:
USL is the Upper Specification Limit
LSL is the Lower Specification Limit
μ is the process Mean
σ_ω (Standard Deviation) is estimated as follows:

$$\sigma_\omega = \frac{\bar{R}}{d_2}$$

As $\bar{x}$ is the average of our measurements, $\bar{R}$ is the average of our Range calculations. Putting a bar over a quantity simply means taking an average of that quantity. An example of the manual process follows:

The table below summarizes some hypothetical process measurements. We will assume that it is data gathered from measuring dimension "R" on a machined part. The process was sampled on six different occasions with each sample consisting of five separate measurements.

	Sample1	Sample2	Sample3	Sample4	Sample5	Sample6
Measurement 1	0.84925	0.84930	0.84875	0.84820	0.84835	0.84925
Measurement 2	0.84925	0.84890	0.84875	0.84845	0.84825	0.84890
Measurement 3	0.84945	0.84970	0.84850	0.84975	0.84880	0.84850
Measurement 4	0.84935	0.84965	0.84855	0.84815	0.84875	0.84815
Measurement 5	0.84940	0.84995	0.84915	0.84825	0.84860	0.84860
Sum	4.24670	4.24750	4.24370	4.24280	4.24275	4.24340
Average (X-Bar)	0.84934	0.84950	0.84874	0.84856	0.84855	0.84868
MAX	0.84945	0.84995	0.84915	0.84975	0.84880	0.84925
MIN	0.84925	0.84890	0.84850	0.84815	0.84825	0.84815
RANGE (MAX-MIN)	0.00020	0.00105	0.00065	0.00160	0.00055	0.00110

We will also assume that our customer has defined the LSL and USL of this particular dimension as 0.8347 and 0.8582 respectively.

Since sampling consisted of five separate measurements, our sample size (or N) is five, we use the previous Select Unbiasing Constants table to look up the appropriate value for d_2 and find that it is 2.326.

Using the data in the above table, CP, CPU, CPL, and Cpk are calculated as follows:

$$CP = \frac{(USL - LSL)}{6\sigma_\omega}, \quad \sigma_\omega = \frac{\bar{R}}{d_2}$$

$$\sigma_\omega = \frac{\bar{R}}{d_2}$$

$$\sigma_\omega = \frac{0.00086}{2.326}$$

$$\sigma_\omega = 0.000369 (rounded)$$

$$CP = \frac{(USL - LSL)}{6\sigma_\omega}$$

$$CP = \frac{(0.8582 - 0.8347)}{6(0.000369)}$$

$$CP = 10.613786$$

$$Cpk = min[CPU, CPL]$$

$$CPU = \frac{(USL - \mu)}{3\sigma_\omega} \text{ and } CPL = \frac{(\mu - LSL)}{3\sigma_\omega}$$

$$CPU = \frac{(0.8582 - 0.848895)}{3(0.000369)}$$

$$and$$

$$CPL = \frac{(0.848895 - 0.8347)}{3(0.000369)}$$

$$CPU = 8.405216 \text{ and } CPL = 12.822357$$

$$Cpk = 8.405216$$

The preceding example calculations were performed in Excel® and are available for review in the EZ SPC.xlsx file in the Cpk tab. However, the manual calculations are quite tedious. It is much easier and less error prone to use a software package such as Minitab® where a few mouse clicks will automatically perform the calculations and produce a graphical summary as shown on the next page.

Process Capability of Dimension "R"

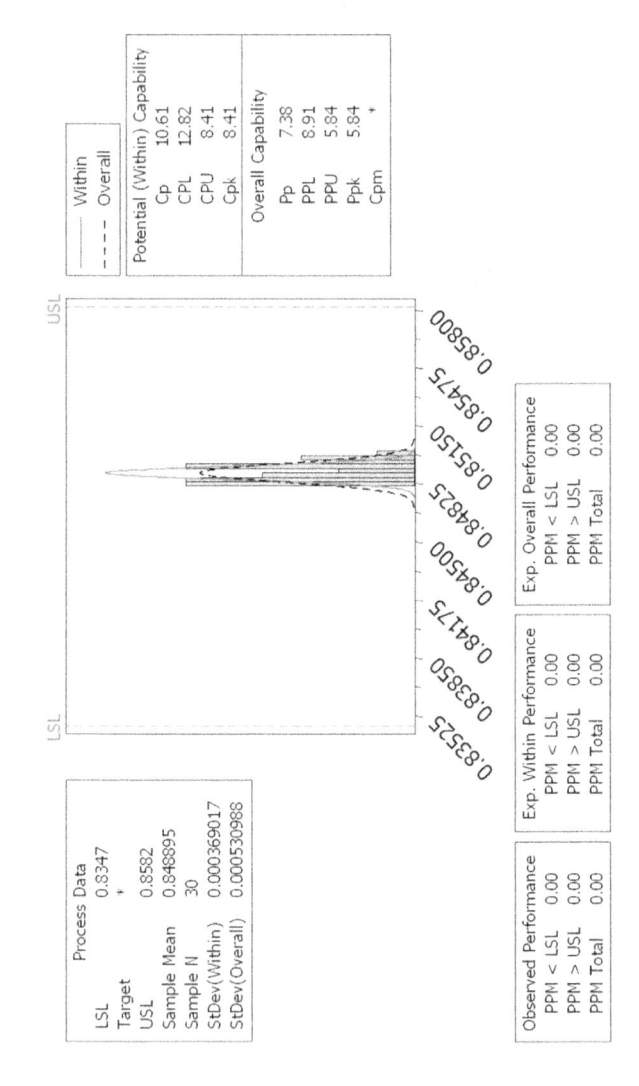

Process Data
LSL 0.8347
Target *
USL 0.8582
Sample Mean 0.848895
Sample N 30
StDev(Within) 0.000369017
StDev(Overall) 0.000530988

Potential (Within) Capability
Cp 10.61
CPL 12.82
CPU 8.41
Cpk 8.41

Overall Capability
Pp 7.38
PPL 8.91
PPU 5.84
Ppk 5.84
Cpm *

Observed Performance
PPM < LSL 0.00
PPM > USL 0.00
PPM Total 0.00

Exp. Within Performance
PPM < LSL 0.00
PPM > USL 0.00
PPM Total 0.00

Exp. Overall Performance
PPM < LSL 0.00
PPM > USL 0.00
PPM Total 0.00

In the Control Limits section of this book, I said that the Control Limits were dictated by the Standard Deviation of the process. Now, knowing that there are mathematical relationships between Cpk, Standard Deviation, Spec. Limits, and Control Limits we can use this knowledge to back into a set of maximum allowable Control Limits that will allow us to meet our process Cpk requirements before the process is even begun. The calculations for LCL and UCL would be as follows:

$$UCL = \frac{USL - LSL}{2} + LSL + \frac{USL - \left[\frac{USL - LSL}{2} + LSL\right]}{C_{pk}}$$

$$LCL = \frac{USL - LSL}{2} + LSL - \frac{\left[\frac{USL - LSL}{2} + LSL\right] - LSL}{C_{pk}}$$

These calculations assume that the target value of the process is midway between the LSL and USL. These calculations are already setup for your use in the EZ SPC.xlsx file on the LCL-UCL tab. These calculations should only be used to create the initial Control Charts in the absence of any real process data as they allow for the widest possible Control Limits that meet the Cpk specification. Our goal is to continually work to minimize variation in the process, always narrowing the Control Limits.

Ralph V. Celone

CHAPTER 17

Ralph V. Celone

CHAPTER 17
Z SCORES

Customers may also dictate their process quality requirements as Z Scores. Z Scores are another measure of Process Capability. There are two types of Z Scores, Long-term and Short-term. The theory is that process performance will be better when measured on a short-term basis. The Long-term and Short-term scores are written as Z_{LT} and Z_{ST} respectively. Z_{ST} Scores can be calculated by multiplying the Cpk times 3. Z_{LT} is simply 1.5 less than Z_{ST}. When people specify Z Score requirements, they are typically calling out Z_{ST}, but it's best to ask if it's not specified. Like Ppk and Cpk, Z Scores can take on negative values. Also like Ppk and Cpk, negative values mean you are producing more defects than acceptable outputs from the process being measured. Other terms that are mathematically related to Z Scores and Cpk are the Probability Density Function (PDF), Yield, and Defects Per Million

Opportunities (DPMO).

A simplified explanation of the PDF is that it is the probability that any random process output will be within the Specification Limits of the process.

Yield is the percentage of process outputs that can be expected to be within the Specification Limits of the process and is the PDF expressed as a percentage.

DPMO is the number of process outputs that can be expected to be outside the Specification Limits of the process per million samples.

In Excel® the NORMSDIST and NORMSINV functions can be used to calculate the PDF, Z Scores and Cpk given a specific sample size and the number of defects in that sample. The use of these functions is demonstrated in the Z-Score tab of the companion Excel® file. That tab also has a Z Score/Cpk calculator to use with your own process data.

The following table shows the relationship between Cpk, Z Scores, the PDF, Process Yield, and Process DPMO.

DPMO	Z-Score$_{LT}$	Z-Score$_{ST}$	Cpk	PDF	Yield
691,300	-0.50	1.00	0.33	0.308700	30.8700%
308,537	0.50	2.00	0.67	0.691463	69.1463%
66,807	1.50	3.00	1.00	0.933193	93.3193%
6,200	2.50	4.00	1.33	0.993800	99.3800%
232	3.50	5.00	1.67	0.999768	99.9768%
3.4	4.50	6.00	2.00	0.999997	99.9997%

Again, process quality requirements may be called as a Cpk (1.67), a Z Score (5.00), a yield (99.9768%), or Defects Per Million Opportunities (232) – they are all equivalent measures.

There may not appear to be much difference between a Z Score of 4.00, 5.00, or 6.00, or it may not seem worth the effort to bring your quality to the next level. To put that into perspective, consider this: According to wiki.answers.com, there are about 33,000 flights in and out of JFK every month. If we were to measure successful take-offs and landings, at a Z Score of 4.00, we would see about 204 crashes each month. At a Z Score of 5.00, we would see about 7 or 8 crashes each month. At a Z Score of 6.00, we would see a crash about every 9 months.

All of the previous tables and calculations are focused on answering a single question: "What is the chance that any random output from the process will be within the Specification Limits?" Our goal is to make that chance as high as possible.

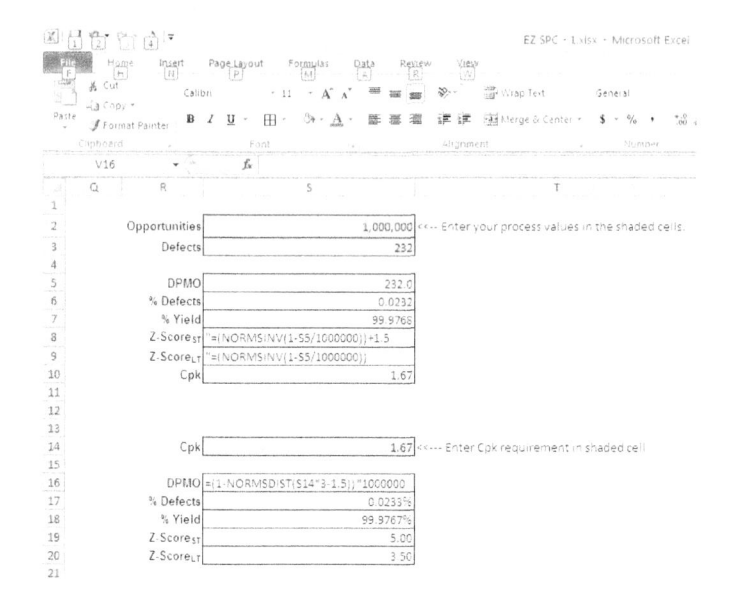

Opportunities	1,000,000	<<--- Enter your process values in the shaded cells
Defects	232	
DPMO	232.0	
% Defects	0.0232	
% Yield	99.9768	
Z-Score$_{ST}$	=(NORMSINV(1-S5/1000000))+1.5	
Z-Score$_{LT}$	=(NORMSINV(1-S5/1000000))	
Cpk	1.67	

Cpk	1.67	<<--- Enter Cpk requirement in shaded cell
DPMO	=(1-NORMSDIST(S14*3-1.5))*1000000	
% Defects	0.0233%	
% Yield	99.9767%	
Z-Score$_{ST}$	5.00	
Z-Score$_{LT}$	3.50	

Syntax of NORMSINV & NORMSDIST

CHAPTER 18

Ralph V. Celone

CHAPTER 18
IMPLEMENTATION

The first phase of the implementation should consist of training programs for the people who will be given the duties of taking the measurements, performing the calculations and updating the charts.

This book and the accompanying Excel® file were generated from the SPC training programs I have previously developed and would make an excellent base for your own training program.

The key to a successful training program is to connect the theory to the practical as quickly as possible and to repeat the exercises until everyone in the training class understands how to perform the calculations. Start the training program with the M&M® measurements mentioned earlier in this book. Use the Excel® file to introduce the new calculations and then move on to practicing the more advanced techniques with measurements from your own operation.

The initial rollout should be based around paper charts that are manually completed and displayed where the process is performed. It is very important that the initial rollout is a manual system to reinforce the connection between the process, the measurements, the calculations, and the SPC chart along with increasing the operator's understanding of the process.

One pitfall to be aware of is that, over time, the tendency is to automate the measurements, calculations and chart plotting. This creates a perceived shift in responsibility from the operators who make actual measurements, create graphs and actually control the process to QA inspectors who only check a computer screen and have no direct control over the process. For the people controlling the process, this breaks the connections between the SPC chart and the process output. At that point, SPC becomes just one more thing to do and the insight into the process performance is lost. To prevent this from happening, you have two choices. Either stick with the manual, paper-based system or invest in continual training and reinforcement for the operators. While the paper-based method is great for maintaining the link between operator and process, an electronic system is great for historical data storage and archival.

I have always opted for a paper-based rollout for two reasons: the initial costs are very low and it creates that important link between operator and process. Once the connection becomes part of the culture, I have gone on to electronic systems, but have always required the people controlling the process to also be assigned the tasks of taking the process measurements and entering the process data. I have always pushed for continual training to reinforce the cultural change.

CHAPTER 19

Ralph V. Celone

CHAPTER 19
A FEW WORDS ABOUT FMEA

Even though it doesn't directly tie to SPC, a few words about Failure Mode and Effects Analysis (FMEA) are in order. FMEA can be used to assess the risk of failure associated with a process defect and to prioritize the deployment of resources to minimize the risk. FMEA is another technique that is not well explained in most literature but can be easily understood.

Basically, an FMEA is taking a particular mode of failure, or a particular manner in which a defect can occur, and estimating the Probability of Occurrence, the Severity of the Failure, and the difficulty of Detecting the failure. These estimates are generally multiplied in a spreadsheet to determine a risk associated with that failure mode. There are several scoring methods for each parameter.

A typical scoring method for Probability of Occurrence might be 1, 2, or 3 corresponding to "Low", "Medium", or "High". Another might be 1, 2, 3, 4, or 5 corresponding to "Almost Impossible", "Remote", "Occasional", "Multiple Failures", or "Almost Certain to Fail". Another possibility is ranking on a 1 to 10 scale. The general idea is that the more likely a failure is to occur, the higher the score is that gets assigned to it.

Likewise, the scoring method for Severity follows the same general rule. The more severe the failure, the higher the Severity is scored. On the low end of the scale would be "No Effect on Reliability or Safety" and on the high end of the scale would be "Multiple Deaths or Severe Financial Consequences" – you divide the scale as finely as desired as long as you are consistent.

Lastly, we need to score Difficulty of Detection on a numerical scale. The low end of the scale would be something like "Certain to be Detected Before Affecting the Customer". The high end of the scale would be along the lines of "Unable to be Detected by Manufacturer or Customer Until Failure Occurs".

Let's imagine that we are building rotor blades for a helicopter. A simplified explanation of the basic construction is a skin of several layers of composite materials like fiberglass, kevlar, and graphite bonded to an expanded honeycomb core. This build up is bonded to a titanium spar. Let's imagine that the failure mode we're considering is a disbond from the titanium spar caused by contamination of the spar after cleaning. The current spar cleaning process consists of an acid bath and a deionized water rinse. The spar is then loaded onto a cart and trucked to the assembly area.

Probability of Occurrence: After mapping out the process, we find that the spar is cleaned in an area of the plant that is diagonally opposite the blade assembly area. To get from one corner to the other, the forklift driver must tow the cart of cleaned spars through the machine shop area. At times the air in the machine shop is saturated with oil from the various machining processes and our adhesive cannot bond to an oily surface. We are forced to rank the Probability of Occurrence as High on our 1 to 3 scale.

Severity: Should the blade disbond during flight, the effect would most likely be Multiple Deaths and Severe Financial Consequences. Again, we are forced to rank this as High on our 1 to 3 scale.

Detection: Currently, we have no valid way to detect an improper bond during the manufacturing process. We need to score this high because this defect is "Unable to be Detected by Manufacturer or Customer Until Failure Occurs".

We continue on with other possible failures for this assembly, put the numbers into a spreadsheet and obtain the following:

Failure Mode	Probability of Occurrence	Severity	Difficulty of Detection	Risk
Disbond from Spar	3	3	3	27
Failure 2	1	2	3	6
Failure 3	3	2	1	6
Failure 4	2	2	3	12
etc.				

Using our Low, Medium, High ranking system, we cannot possibly score the disbond risk any higher and must take action to reduce the risk. We could move the blade assembly area next to the spar cleaning area and eliminate the trip through the machine shop. We could cover the spar with some type of protective barrier after cleaning. We could purchase some type of X-Ray inspection system to check the assembly after it's completed. Any of these actions (and there are probably others) would reduce our risk.

As multiple Failure Modes are included in the spreadsheet, it can also be utilized to prioritize the use of resources to attack the highest risk failures first.

The only other consideration is a cost/benefit analysis. This naturally leads to the next step of mistake-proofing your processes. For a great mistake-proofing reference, see "No Eraser Needed" by Ronald L. Buckley.

CHAPTER 20

Ralph V. Celone

CHAPTER 20
CONCLUSION

Don't just read this book and put it on a shelf. Go out into the factory or the office, train others, get people involved, start taking measurements and defining acceptable standards and you will see an overall performance improvement, happier customers, and lower operating costs.

But remember to make it fun and interesting – use plenty of M&Ms® and lots of real-world examples that your people can relate to.

SPC Terms and Definitions

Ralph V. Celone

# SPC Terms and Definitions

Average, Mean or $\overline{x}$	All three of these terms mean the same thing. The sum of measurements in a sample divided by the number of items measured
LSL, USL	Lower Spec. Limit & Upper Spec. Limit – tolerance limits on a dimension, or other process parameter, allowed by a customer
LCL, UCL	Lower Control Limit & Upper Control Limit – tolerance limits allowed on a process parameter as dictated by the process – not to be confused with LSL & USL – a measurement could be within the spec. limits but the process could still be out of control – LCL & UCL are much tighter than the LSL & USL
Median	The middle value of a set of measurements
Mode	The most common value of a set of measurements

SPC Terms and Definitions

Range   The difference between the smallest and largest measurements

R Chart   The chart that is used to plot the range of a set of measurements

Standard Deviation   The "spread" or variation of measurements around the average value

Histogram   A graphical display of tabulated frequencies

Trend   An indication that something is drifting towards an "out of control" condition – generally seven points in a row on one side of the average or seven points in a row consistently increasing or decreasing or Cycling

Cycling   When a process measurement varies back and forth in a regular pattern – this is an indication that something is causing an "out of control" condition – all drifting should be random patterns

SPC Terms and Definitions

$\bar{x}$ Chart The chart that is used to plot the average of a set of measurements

Cp, Cpk Process Capability, Process Capability Index. Indicator of process capability. Used when sampling a population. Used to predict future process outcomes.

Pp, Ppk Process Performance, Process Performance Index. Indicators of actual process performance. Used to quantify historical performance. Especially useful to quantify process improvements.

Z Score A measure of Process Capability that can be used to set the expectations of the number of "good" and "bad" outputs from a process.

Ralph V. Celone

Sources

iSixSigma.com, 2011 – 2013

GE internal Six Sigma training materials, 2000 – 2006

Introduction to Statistical Quality Control, D. C. Montgomery, 2001

Probability and Statistics for Engineers and Scientists, Walpole, Myers and Myers, 1998

Basic Statistical Process Control, David W. Simmerer, 1993

Mathematical Statistics, John E. Freund/Ronald E. Walpole, 1987

Ralph V. Celone

ABOUT THE AUTHOR

Author Ralph Celone holds a Bachelor's degree in Electrical Engineering and a Master's degree in Business Administration. He has been studying process modeling and improvement for most of his 30+ year career while actively employing those techniques in many successful Lean conversions. He has had the pleasure of working for some of world's greatest companies like General Electric and United Technologies in various leadership roles. His career has spanned many diverse industries, including semiconductor manufacturing, aerospace, medical electronics, wire & cable, healthcare and many more. One of the author's most important talents is the ability to take very complex topics and break them down into easily understandable, bite-sized pieces. That is what this book does for SPC – in fact, one of the proofreaders was the author's daughter who had not yet graduated High School. With no previous knowledge of Statistical Process Control, she was able to master the techniques illustrated in this book.

Ralph V. Celone

Ralph V. Celone

Ralph V. Celone